Microsoft Access

Bible

Microsoft Access

Bible

By

Jason Taylor

3

TABLE OF CONTENTS

4

5

7

8

INTRODUCTION

Compared to other Office apps like Word, Excel, and PowerPoint, Microsoft Access is known for being harder to learn and operate. There exist several explanations for this, and gaining a solid comprehension of Microsoft Access can be really beneficial in comprehending the various tasks that this robust software can do.

HOW ACCESS IS DISTINCTIVE

When using Office, you can start creating something useful almost instantly and directly on the screen with Word, Excel, and PowerPoint. However, when using Access, you have to first design and create structures to hold your data before creating unique template layouts for manipulating, displaying, and presenting that data in a meaningful and useful way. Put another way, Access needs more careful consideration, careful planning, and well-designed interfaces in order to be used efficiently, as opposed to being created haphazardly. Although Access involves a lot of "learn by doing," there is a lot you should know before you use it.

THE OPERATION OF ACCESS

In essence, Access gives you the following two options:

- It enables you to keep enormous volumes of data.

9

- It enables you to work with that data to create pertinent and helpful information. This is the main purpose of database management systems (DBMS), and Access is fortunately one of the simplest to use and understand.

Tables are used to store data. Tables are structures consisting of rows and columns that function similarly to Excel worksheets in terms of appearance. The tables must be designed and made by you before any data can be submitted.

Table data can be modified through the use of forms, reports, and queries. Though data can also be entered directly into a table, forms are typically used for data input tasks. A report is used to change the data and show it in a more aesthetically acceptable manner, either on the computer or written on paper. To generate a subset of the data, a query is utilized. For instance, in a sales system, you might want to view only the sales in the northwest.

Layout frameworks are used to generate forms, reports, and queries. The data from the tables can then be run through the framework once it has been constructed. Yes, design versus display is a recurring theme in Microsoft Access. In design mode, you build or edit a form, report, or query; in display mode, you preview the data. Tables—which house your

10

data—also follow this design/display parable. After creating a table structure, you input the data into a display view, also known as a datasheet view.

Database objects include queries, forms, reports, and tables. Actually, every single one of these functions as a miniature version of the larger Access application. You can construct the structure or framework and show data using the vast array of commands and settings available in each.

WHAT USES DOES ACCESS HAVE?

Access can be used to establish a system for keeping track of your sales at work, your music or stamp collection, your membership in the local polo or soccer club, petty cash, inventory, and stock control, among many other things. Access is a great option for any scenario in where you need to store data, process it, and then display it as informative.

The main drawback of Access is that you have to plan and construct the system as well as the database objects (tables, forms, reports, and queries) that are used in it, unless you use one of the pre-made system templates. It takes time and knowledge to accomplish this.

11

CHAPTER ONE

GETTING STARTED WITH THE PC

Microsoft Access must be opened in order to create a new database or work with an existing one. When you launch Access for the first time, it must open from either the Start menu's All programs list or the taskbar's Search the web and Windows bar. To make it easier and faster to access the next time you need it, you can opt to pin it to the taskbar or the Start menu.

Give It a Try:

- Make sure your computer is turned on and the desktop is visible before starting.
- In the event that the taskbar at the bottom of the desktop is devoid of an Access icon, select the Windows icon to bring up the Start menu.
- To see a list of every app on your computer, click All apps. To reach the A section, scroll down.
- To begin, click Access.
- To see a menu of options, right-click on the Access icon in the taskbar, as shown. Then, choose Pin this program to taskbar.

12

This icon can now be clicked to launch Access on the desktop. Until removed, this icon will stay in the taskbar. To reopen Access, click the Access icon in the taskbar.

COMPREHENDING THE START SCREEN

When you launch Access, most of the time a start screen appears. You can choose the type of database you wish to work with right from this first screen. You have the option of opening a database that has been saved to Computer or OneDrive, working with one of your most recently viewed

13

files, or starting from scratch with one of the pre-made databases.

START SCREEN OF MICROSOFT ACCESS

If you want to rapidly access a database you have worked on recently or build a new database based on one of the various templates (including the default Blank desktop database), the Microsoft Access start screen is really beneficial.

A list of recent databases will appear beneath Recent in the pane to the left of the screen if you have previously worked on one or more databases in Access. You can still access databases that you have already worked on by selecting the Open Other Files link, which is found beneath Recent. This allows you to open an existing file from OneDrive or your computer.

The start screen's main pane shows you the available templates for building a new database, along with a search box to look up more templates online. Templates are essentially pre-made layouts that you may modify to fit your requirements and add pertinent material to. The Blank desktop database template is an option if you want to start from scratch; you'll probably discover that this is the one you use the most. The globe-icon templates (like Asset tracking) host your database online using web-based SharePoint

14

servers; please take aware that these templates need to be subscribed to.

The account information that you used to log into Windows, together with help, minimize, restore, and close options, are located in the upper right corner of the screen.

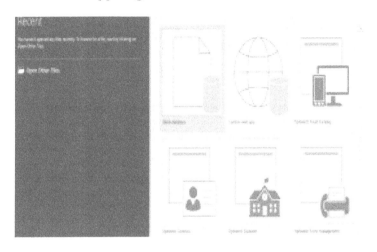

MAKING A NEW DATABASE, BLANK

The start page that appears when you install Microsoft Access allows you to open an existing database or create a new one using a variety of accessible templates. The majority of the templates on display are web-based and could require an Office 365 subscription. Another option is to just make a fresh, blank desktop database, which is free.

15

Make sure the Access Start screen appears before beginning this exercise.

- On the Blank desktop database option in the right pane. You'll be required to give the database a name.
- Double-click C:/ Course Files for Microsoft Access and select [OK] after typing My Database in File Name and selecting the Browse icon to open the File New Database dialog box.

We'll go with the blank template, but you can click the Next arrow to see the various pre-made templates and use one of those instead.

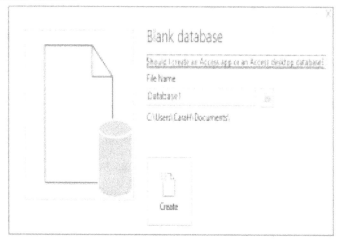

- To open the new, blank database in Access, click [Create].

16

Access has initially created one blank table for you.

COMMUNICATING WITH THE BACKSTAGE VIEW

Database files need to be open in order for Microsoft Access to function properly. Your database objects (tables, forms,

THE BACKSTAGE AREA

The File tab is not a typical ribbon tab. When the File tab is clicked, Microsoft Access opens as a mini-program known as **Backstage view**, or just **Backstage**.

The left portion of the Backstage is taken up by a navigation window. You can do several activities, such printing and saving, using the options in this pane. You can also obtain details about your database, like its size. To adjust the

17

display in the pane on the right, click on the choices located in the navigation pane.

Info	gives status information about the current database and allows you to condense, fix, and password-protect the database.
New	gives you the ability to build a new database and gives you quick access to a variety of online templates in addition to built-in templates.
Open	offers a list of recently uploaded documents along with the ability to search your computer, SkyDrive, or other location for the document.
Save	keeps your active object (form, query, table, etc.) saved.
Save As	allows you to save the current database in a different location and/or format (such as .mdb, which is compatible with versions older than 2007).
Print	allows you to preview and print the currently selected object.
Close	closes the database you are currently using.
Account	includes data on the product and the user.

Options	opens the Access Options dialog box, where you may adjust the basic Access settings as well as the preferences for the active database.
Feedback	enables you to give Microsoft feedback on any problems or recommendations you may have with Access.

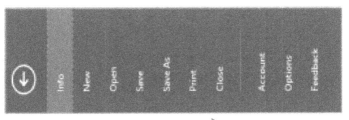

19

CHAPTER TWO

ACCESSING AN OLD DATABASE FILE

Access can be effectively shown by opening an existing database file. You must utilize the Backstage's Open option in order to open a database file. The database file can show up in the Recent Database list if it has recently been opened.

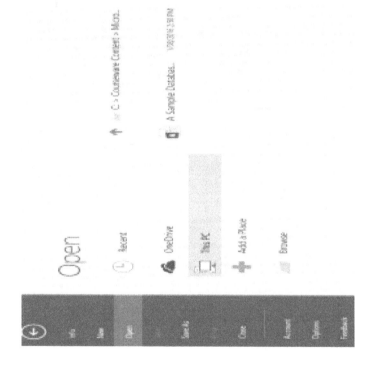

You'll have to look for and open it using one of the other Open options if it doesn't show up there.

20

ACCEPTING THE ACCESS SCREEN

An Access database interface appears to be rather simple at first sight. You can actually only do one of the following actions on the screen: create, edit, or execute a database

object (tables, forms, reports, queries, etc.) within a database file. The screen doesn't actually get more complicated unless

21

you decide to carry out one of these operations. The tabbed band that runs across the top of the window is called the **ribbon**. It is Access's central command and control center. Commands that have been grouped together can be accessed via the ribbon's tabs. Commands can take the shape of buttons or occasionally include galleries with many formatting options for you to choose from. When a database object is opened, this area truly comes to life. To access file management features like saving, opening, closing, printing, etc., select the File tab on the ribbon. You may also customize your working preferences and Access choices by using the ribbon.

The data section occupies the majority of the screen. In this case, a database object will show up in preview or design mode. Asset Items in the screen above is selected, but it hasn't been opened yet because the database object needs to be opened before it can be seen.

The different database items (tables, forms, reports, queries, etc.) that are present in the database are listed and navigated using the **Navigation pane**. All objects are displayed by default (as seen above), but you may filter the pane to show only certain types of objects, like tables, if you'd like. Details on the database object that is open at the moment are

22

shown in the Security and Message section. The space is not displaying much right now other than the fact that it is prepared for you to start since there are no things visible.

APPLYING THE RIBBON

Access's command center is the ribbon. It offers a number of commands arranged in groups and displayed on pertinent tabs. Clicking on a tab's name causes the command groups to appear.

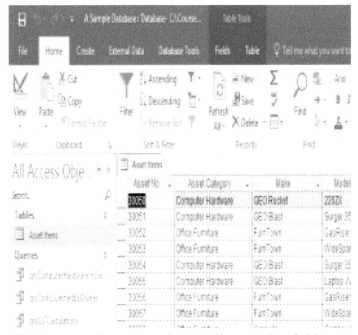

Clicking on a button, tool, or gallery option initiates a command.

23

The ribbon offers a clear, easy way to access options, even if there are frequently other ways to do so.

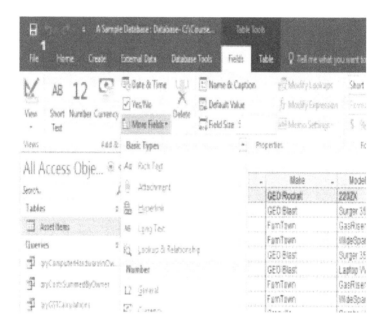

OPERATING THE NAVIGATION PANEL

Because it gives you access to the database objects in your database file, the Navigation pane is a crucial component of Access. Before you start creating tables and other database items, you should have a solid understanding of how the pane itself works. It can be filtered to show you more or less objects.

24

Give It a Try:

- Click the All Access Objects drop arrow in the Navigation pane, as indicated. It will display a menu.

- Choose Queries from the Filter By Group option to view solely the database's saved query objects.

- To view just the reports, click the drop arrow once more and choose Reports.

- To view every database object, click the drop arrow once more and choose All Access Objects.

- In the Navigation window, click the arrow to the right of Forms. The arrows will become double down arrows and the shapes will become obscured.

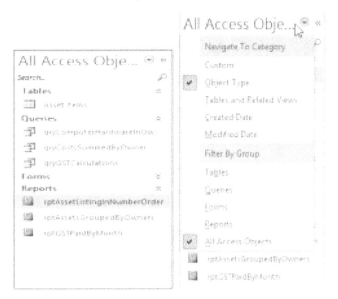

25

- To see the forms once more, click the arrow to the right of the word "Forms."

CHAPTER THREE

INCLUDING DIRECTIONS IN THE QUICK ACCESS TOOLBAR

The Quick Access Toolbar, or QAT for short, is a little toolbar that sits in the upper left corner of the Access window. It's a useful spot to keep the ribbon commands that you use the most often. Locating the command, performing a right-click, and choosing Add to Quick Access Toolbar are the steps involved in adding commands from the ribbon.

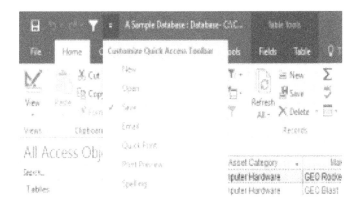

Do It Yourself

You have two options for completing this exercise: open A Sample Database or continue with the previous file.

- To view the tool's name and shortcut, point to the first button on the Quick Access Toolbar. In our instance,

27

it's the Save tool; by default, the QAT only displays the Save, Undo, and Redo tools.

- To see a shortcut menu, right-click on Filter in the Sort & Filter group on the Home tab.

HOW TO ADD A FILTER TOOL ON QUICK ACCESS TOOLBAR

- To add the Filter tool to the Quick Access Toolbar (QAT), select Add.

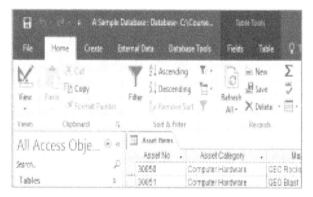

- To view a menu, click Customize Quick Access Toolbar, as indicated.
- To add the Open tool to the QAT, select Open. The process of removing unwanted tools from the QAT is equally simple.
- In the QAT, right-click the Filter tool, then choose Remove from Quick Access Toolbar.

28

- To remove the Open tool from the QAT, repeat step again.

UTILIZING TOUCH MODE

These days, a lot of people use Office apps on touchscreen gadgets like smartphones and tablets. These panels are tiny, so it's simple to inadvertently touch the wrong command. You can help avoid this by turning on touch mode, which increases the distance between ribbon commands, QAT tools, and ribbon tabs.

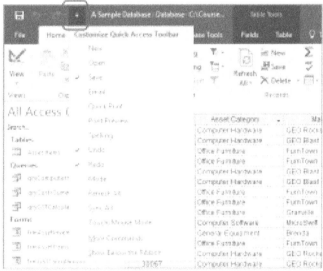

Give It a Try:

- Use the preceding file to carry out this exercise going forward, or open A Sample Database. As shown

29

below, click Customize Quick Access Toolbar. Choose the Mouse/Touch Mode.

- This won't actually turn on Touch mode; it will just add the tool to the Quick Access toolbar.

- To access a menu, select Touch/Mouse Mode in the

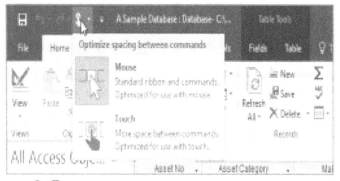

QAT.

- Default is set to mouse mode. The commands are optimized for mouse use in this mode.

- Choose Touch.

There will be a major dispersion of the ribbon's tabs, commands, and Quick Access toolbar capabilities. Now let's go back to the standard Mouse mode. To activate Mouse mode, repeat steps and choose Mouse. The tool should be taken off of the Quick Access toolbar. In the QAT, right-click on Touch/Mouse Mode and choose the option to remove it from the Quick Access Toolbar.

30

A DATABASE FILE CLOSING

Closing a file in a database differs slightly from most other programs. Changes made to structures and designs in Access database files are saved when the objects are closed, however data inserted into the file is saved immediately. As a result, nothing will ever ask you to save new data that is added to a database file—all of this is done automatically.

Give It a Try:

31

- Use the preceding file to carry out this exercise going forward, or open A Sample Database.
- To access the Backstage, select the File tab.
- To exit the database and go back to the Home tab, select Close.
- You closed the database; thus, the Home tab is the one that is selected. Access only allows one database to be open at a time, and while a database is not open, Access always shows the Home tab.

CHAPTER FOUR

HOW TO CREATE A NEW DATABASE FILE

All of your database's components—tables, reports, forms, and the like—are kept together in a single file in Access that has the extension ACCDB. This is the file that is often called the database; it should not be confused with the tables that hold your data. A new database file must be created before any tables, reports, forms, or other objects can be created.

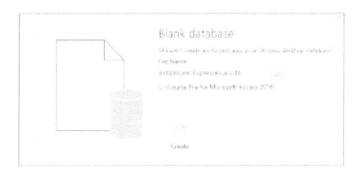

Give It a Try:

- Access is launched before you start.
- The start screen is now visible; if not, select the File tab to bring up the New area in the Backstage.
- To enter "employee expenses", click the Blank desktop database template and type the text. We'll store it in the same location as the other course files.

33

- The File New Database dialog box will appear when you click the Browse icon.
- Next, find and double-click the Course Files for Microsoft Access folder, then select [OK]. The database will now be saved in the course files folder.
- To start creating the new database, click [Create].
- To close the automatically displayed table click the Close button.

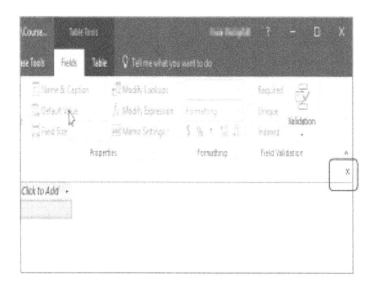

GENERATING THE LOOKUP TABLE

The records that the transaction table will search through are stored in the lookup table. Employee records are stored in the lookup table in this case. The fields in the table must be

34

created, together with their size and type, in order to create a lookup table. The employee information that is required for our database but unrelated to particular spending transactions will be stored in the fields.

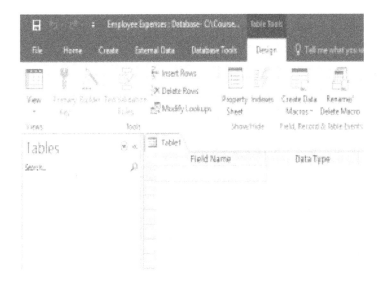

Give It a Try:

- To display a new table, select the Create tab and then click Table Design in the Tables group.

- In Field Name, type EmpNo, then push for the sake of the Data Type.

- Select the Data Type drop-down menu, select Short Text if needed, and then push to go to the Description screen. Type the employee number.

35

- Select the value for Field Size and type 6 in the Field Properties section located at the bottom of the window.

- To begin a new field, click in the row under EmpNo. Then, repeat steps 2 through 5 to construct the remaining fields as indicated.

Field Name	Data Type	Description (Optional)
EmpNo	Short Text	Records the employee number
FirstName	Short Text	Records the employee's first name
LastName	Short Text	Records the employee's family name
Department	Short Text	Record's the employee's department
Started	Date/Time	Record's the employee's starting date
DateOfBirth	Date/Time	Records the employee's date of birth
FullTime	Yes/No	Records employment status
WeeklyHours	Number	Records the normal weekly hours
Salary	Currency	Records the employee's annual salary
Comments	Long Text	Records comments about the employee

- For the next task, leave the table design displayed on the screen.

DEFINING THE PRIMARY KEY

A lookup database needs to be able to obtain data quickly and conveniently in order to be of any use. It must also be able to quickly gather information by combining data from several tables. Each table needs to have a field, or collection of fields, that uniquely identifies each entry in order to enable this. The primary key is this field or group of fields.

36

Give It a Try:

- Make sure the table design from the previous task is displayed before beginning this one.

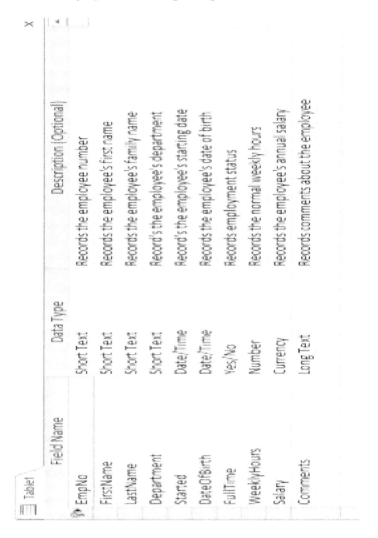

Field Name	Data Type	Description (Optional)
EmpNo	Short Text	Records the employee number
FirstName	Short Text	Records the employee's first name
LastName	Short Text	Records the employee's family name
Department	Short Text	Record's the employee's department
Started	Date/Time	Record's the employee's starting date
DateOfBirth	Date/Time	Records the employee's date of birth
FullTime	Yes/No	Records employment status
WeeklyHours	Number	Records the normal weekly hours
Salary	Currency	Records the employee's annual salary
Comments	Long Text	Records comments about the employee

- A key symbol designates a primary key.

37

- To pick the field, click EmpNo in Field Name. Click the Primary Key option under the Tools group on the Table Tools: Design tab.

To let you know that this is the major key field, a tiny key icon will appear to the left of the field as seen above.

For the next task, leave the table design displayed on the screen.

SAVE AND CLOSE A TABLE

Tables are objects that need to be saved if you wish to keep any design modifications you make, as contrast to data that is saved as you leave a field. The table can be saved while you work on it or when you close it. One benefit of this procedure is that you may easily close the table without saving it if you wish to go back to the original configurations.

Give It a Try

- Make sure the table design from the previous task is displayed before beginning this one.
- To see the Save As dialog box, click the File tab and choose Save. Since we are only saving an object inside the database and the Save As options apply to the database as a whole, we chose to save rather than save as.

38

- This Save As dialog box is rather little in comparison to the larger ones seen in other applications.

This is so that there is no need to specify a file location for database objects because the table structure is saved as part of the database file.

- After entering Employees in Table Name, select [OK].

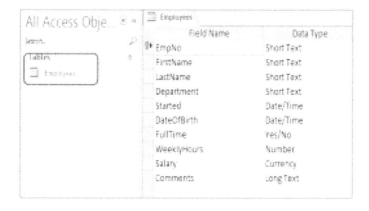

- The table name is now displayed on the table design tab and in the Navigation pane.

39

- To close the table, click Close.

CHAPTER FIVE

FORMING THE TABLE OF TRANSACTIONS

A lookup table that contains the relationships between the individual transactions and a transaction table with the actual transactions make up lookup databases.

Each record in the lookup table may have several entries in the transaction table.

You need to make sure that the transaction table contains the lookup table's main key as a field in order for the relationship to be able to be formed.

Give It a Try

41

- Click the Create tab, then select Table Design in the Tables group to open a new table.

Enter the data as indicated, making sure to change the Description field's Field Size (in Field Properties) to 30.

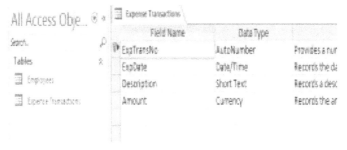

- To make this field the primary key, click on Primary Key in the Tools group after selecting the field by clicking on ExpTransNo in Field Name.
- To open the Save As dialog box, click the Save button on the Quick Access Toolbar.
- Click [OK] after typing Expense Transactions into Table Name.
- To close the table, click the Close button.

The object name now shows in the tab at the top of the design window, and the new table is shown in the Navigation pane.

42

COMPREHENDING THE RELATIONSHIPS OF LOOKUP TABLES

The lookup table and the transaction table are the two necessary tables for a lookup database. These tables need to be associated, or linked in some other way, to function together, according to database terminology. A field that is shared by the two tables is used for this. This is typically the primary key field in the lookup table and the one that is unique.

ONE-TO-MANY CONNECTIONS

A one-to-many link exists between lookup databases. The lookup table in this kind of relationship forms the one side in a one-to-many relationship and contains unique records. Because there could be multiple transactions for each record or entity from the lookup table, the transaction table constitutes the many sides in a one-to-many connection.

Using the Employees database from our case study as an example, this is the lookup table since each employee has a single record here. Each employee may have many records in the Employees table: the Expense Transactions table is the transaction table. The main key in the lookup table is what allows table relationships to exist. In our example, employees are uniquely identified in the table by using the

43

primary key of the Employees table, EmpNo. In order for us to determine who incurred each charge, the relationship must also be present in the charge Transactions database against each transaction. We can use the relationships between the tables to query the data in either table once they have been established.

EmpNo	FirstName	LastName	Department	PhoneNo	Started	Dat
101	Julianne	Kerr	Executive	60001	28-Jun-07	
102	Harry	Jones	Executive	60002	19-Jul-07	
103	Angel	Harrington	Executive	60003	19-Jul-07	
104	Peter	Dawson	Executive	60004	19-Jul-07	
105	Mark	Jones	Executive	60005	19-Jul-07	
106	Maureen	Grayson	Administration	61021	06-Sep-07	
107	Augustine	Milson	Administration	61022	06-Sep-07	

ExpTransNo	ExpDate	Description	Amount	Click to Add
7	2/01/2013	Accommodatic	$125.50	
13	2/01/2013	Meals	$52.86	
14	16/01/2013	Accommodatic	$155.50	
(New)			$0.00	

EmpNo	FirstName	LastName	Department	PhoneNo	Started	Dat
108	Amanda	Bennet	Administration	61023	06-Sep-07	
109	George	Samuelson	Administration	61024	06-Sep-07	
110	Neville	Smith	Administration	61025	06-Sep-07	

LINKING A LOOKUP TABLE

There are several ways to link a transaction table and a lookup table once they have been built.

Creating a Lookup Column in the transaction table using the Lookup Wizard is one of the simplest ways to link the two tables.

44

You can designate which lookup table fields should be presented alongside your transaction data using the wizard.

Screen	Task	Then
1	Select *I want the lookup field to get the values from another table or query*	[Next]
2	Choose *Table:Employees*	[Next]
3	In *Available fields* double-click on *LastName* then on *FirstName*	[Next]
4	Select *LastName* for the first sort column, then *FirstName* for the second sort column, ensuring that both are set to ascending order	[Next]
5	Ensure that *Hide key column* appears with a tick	[Next]
6	Type **Employee** as the label for the lookup field	[Next]

45

Give It a Try

- Make that Design View is turned on. In the Navigation pane, right-click on the Expense Transactions table, then choose Design View if it isn't already active.

- This offers a simple way to show a database object in a certain view.

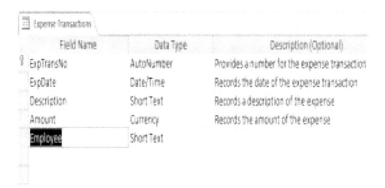

- In the row below the Amount field, click. Finally, to launch the Lookup Wizard, select Modify Lookups in the Tools group on the Table Tools: Design tab.

- Go through the wizard and make the appropriate choices.

- After completing the procedure by selecting [Finish], click [Yes] to save the modifications.

46

- To view the created settings, click the Employee field, then select the Lookup tab in the Field Properties pane. Then, click Close to close the table.

Field Properties

General Lookup

Display Control	Combo Box
Row Source Type	Table/Query
Row Source	SELECT [Employees].[EmpNo], [Employees].[LastName], [Employe
Bound Column	1
Column Count	3
Column Heads	No
Column Widths	0cm;2.54cm;2.54cm
List Rows	16
List Width	5.079cm
Limit To List	Yes
Allow Multiple Values	No
Allow Value List Edits	Yes
List Items Edit Form	
Show Only Row Source V	No

RELATIONSHIPS TABLES

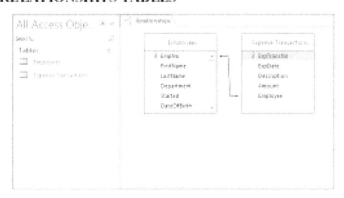

The Relationships pane allows you to examine and modify table relationships you may see more clearly how tables are connected or joined together with the help of this window. To make material easier to find, it also includes a list of every field in every table. You can print a report from the Relationships pane to document a portion of your database architecture.

CHANGING TABLE DESIGNS

ACCESSING AN OLD TABLE

Tables are database objects that are contained in a database file. Working with a table typically involves working with its data, which is accomplished in a unique table view called Datasheet view. Should you wish to

48

If you want to change a table's structure or one of its fields, you have to deal with the table in Design view.

Give It a Try

- Double-clicking the Employees table in the Navigation pane will open it in Datasheet mode.
- To go to Design mode, click on the top half of View in the Views group on the Home tab.

49

- Keep in mind that the View tool's image changes to show which view you will be toggled to. Press View once again to return to Datasheet view.

- To close the table, click the Close button to the right of it.

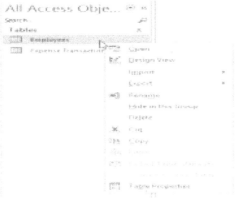

- Right-click the Employees table in the Navigation pane to bring up the shortcut menu. To see the table in Design view, select Design View.

- Shut down the table.

50

CHAPTER SIX

FIELDS ADDITION TO AN EXISTING TABLE

Even though your database design was flawless when you first designed it, after management and end users have reviewed it and even after some more thought or brainstorming, it may become essential for adjusting the field structure.

Thankfully, you can easily add fields to an existing table using contemporary database programs like Access.

51

CHANGING THE SIZE OF THE FIELD

By rights, you ought to have decided on a field's proper size in the design stage. However, under Design view, you can change a field's size at any time. All you have to do is enter a new value in the relevant field's Field Size property to alter the field size.

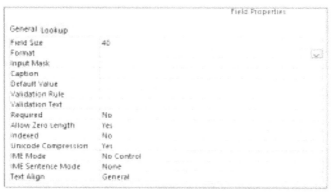

Give It a Try

- To view the Employees table in the Navigation pane, right-click on it and choose Design View.

- Double-click 30 in Field Size in the Field Properties pane at the bottom of the window after selecting the Location field.

- To increase the size, type 40 and press.

- After selecting the PhoneNo field, double-click Field Size.

- Close and save the table.

52

CHANGING THE NAMES OF FIELD

The nomenclature of fields is a topic of significant discussion. Once more, field names are something that should be decided upon before the structure is made and then strictly followed. However, you can quickly modify a field's name in Design mode if necessary.

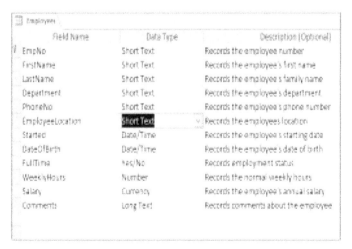

53

Give It a Try

- To view the Employees table in the Navigation pane, right-click on it and choose Design View.

- To put the location field's name in edit mode, double-click on it.

- After typing EmployeeLocation, click

- This name is indicative of a more conventional method of field naming, in which spaces are not used and all words in multi-word names start with a capital letter.

- Close and save the table.

DATE FORMATS CHANGE

There are several reasons why dates might be kept in tables. These could be birth dates, commencement dates, expiration dates, or milestone dates.

You may show dates in Access in a number different forms based on your application's requirements. Long Date,

Medium Date, General Date, Short Date, and other time-only formats are available for selection.

Do It Yourself

To complete this activity, either open the file Modifying Tables or continue using the previous file.

- To view the Employees table in the Navigation pane, right-click on it and choose Design View. To view the Field Properties, click the Started field.
- Click Format in the Field Properties tab, then select Medium Date by clicking the drop arrow.
- For the DateOfBirth field, repeat steps two and three.
- Save the table and Close.

TRANSFERRING A TABLE INTO A DATABASE

It's a good idea to create a backup of the table before making any structural modifications that can cause data loss. Making a duplicate copy of the table inside the database file itself is a quicker and simpler method than backing up the full database file using File Explorer's standard file copy procedures.

Give It a Try

- To copy the Employees table to the clipboard, right-click on it in the Navigation pane and choose Copy.

55

- To view the Paste Table, click the upper portion of Paste in the Clipboard group on the Home tab. as a dialog box appears.

- You can choose what to copy and how to name it using this dialog box.

- To paste a copy of the table, make sure Structure and Data are chosen, then click [OK].
- To put the name in edit mode, right-click on the Copy of Employees table and choose Rename.
- After typing Employees Backup, click Enter.

56

REMOVING A DATABASE FILE'S TABLE

Simply said, tables are items kept in a database file. You may therefore make them, edit them, and even remove them if necessary. The only actual reason to delete a table is, generally speaking, when you no longer need copies of the tables created for data protection and backup.

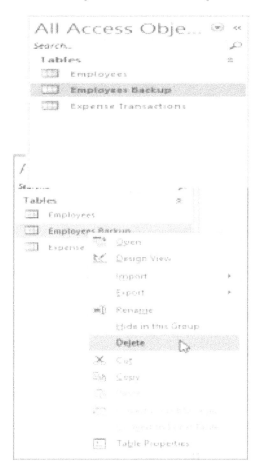

57

- You can either open the file Modifying or carry on with the previous file for this task.
- Right-click the Employees Backup table in the Navigation bar, then choose Delete. A warning about deletion will appear. Select [Yes] to remove the table.

The Navigation pane will no longer display the deleted table.

58

CHAPTER SEVEN

ESTABLISHING RELATIONSHIPS

You can start the process of linking, or joining, the tables together after they have been defined and generated in Microsoft Access.

BENEFITS OF RELATING TABLES

Relating tables has a number of benefits.

- When tables are related, Access enables you to construct multi-table queries that combine the data into a single recordset. This recordset may then be utilized to greatly simplify the process of building intricate reports and forms.

- Access has unique subforms and subdatasheets that facilitate the viewing of relevant data when a relationship has been established between two tables.

- Referential integrity, a set of guidelines that helps stop inaccurate data from entering the tables, can be enforced with connected tables.

COMPREHENDING RELATIONSHIPS IN TABLES

Your data is typically stored in a database consisting of multiple tables in a relational structure. When there are several tables, they are joined or linked together to create a

59

relationship that enables the system to add, edit, or report on the data in the tables as if they were a single unit.

RELATIONSHIP TYPES

Three different kinds of relationships between tables are possible:

- One-to-one
- One-to-many
- Many-to-many

ONE-TO-ONE RELATIONSHIP

This is an uncommon type of relationship in which every record in one table is connected to just one other record in another table.

ONE-TO-MANY RELATIONSHIP

This is the most prevalent type and typically occur when one table is used to search up important information. In this scenario, one record in one table is associated to numerous others in another table. The table with a lot of records in this kind of relationship is frequently called the transaction table, and the other table is called the lookup table since the transaction table uses it to search up data, usually a name, title, or something similar.

60

MANY-TO-MANY RELATIONSHIP

This is incredibly uncommon and difficult; it occurs when many records in one table can be connected to many records in another table.

INTEGRITY OF REFERENCE

The main advantage of connecting tables is most likely referential integrity.

Let's look at two of our system's tables: **Employees** and **Expense** Transactions. There may be numerous expense transaction records for every employee if these tables are connected in a one-to-many fashion.

It would be foolish of our database to allow us to generate a new expenditure transaction without the employee's information as we need to know which employee filed a claim.

It will be impossible to add a new expense record without first assigning it to an employee record that already exists in the Employees database if we impose referential integrity in the one-to-many relationship between the Expense Transactions and Employees tables.

There are other possibilities for referential integrity. For instance, it would be convenient if Access would immediately update the EmpNo number in all associated

61

tables if an employee's number changed. Cascade Update can be enabled to do this.

Likewise, we could want to remove all record of an employee's spending transactions from the system if we remove that individual from the Employees database. You can accomplish this by turning on the Cascade Delete feature, but you should proceed cautiously and carefully consider your company's requirements before doing so. Even if the employee has departed, you might need to keep the cost records for a specific amount of time.

RELATIONSHIPS AS A DATA SECURITY MEASURE

There is a lot of information to take in from this hypothesis. If you examine your data closely, you'll see that these guidelines are merely meant to safeguard it and make sure it stays current and consistent. They also make sure you don't unintentionally erase documents you need to save.

COMPREHENDING LOOKUP CONNECTIONS

Lookups are the most frequent justification for relating tables in a database file. When information from single entity tables needs to be shown in transaction tables, lookups are utilized, typically to help with data entry or reporting. The employee number is used in our case study's costs table, but we must display (i.e., lookup) the employee's name to facilitate data entry.

ONE-TO-MANY CONNECTIONS

The relationship between lookup databases is one-to-many. The lookup table in this kind of relationship forms the one side of the one-to-many relationship and contains unique records. Since each entry or entity from the lookup table may have several transactions, the transaction table represents the many side of the one-to-many relationship.

The transaction table is the source of lookups into the lookup table. Two lookups from the Expense Transactions table are needed for our case study: one for workers and one for expense kinds.

Each employee has a single record in the Employees table, which serves as the lookup table for employees. Each employee may have multiple records in the Expense Transactions table, which is the transaction table. The Expense kinds table is the lookup table for expense kinds: each possible expense type has a single record here. The Expense category table may have numerous records for each category, and the Expense Transactions table is once more the transaction table. The main key in the lookup table is used to enable table relationships. The primary key's

63

functions include maintaining record organization and enabling a quick search system that makes lookups display very instantly. A lookup field, frequently named similarly to the primary key in the lookup table, is used to retrieve the primary key from the transaction table. Once the primary key field in the lookup table has been located using the value in the lookup field, information from additional fields of the discovered record can be utilized.

TABLE RELATIONSHIPS WINDOW

The Relationships window is used to view and modify table relationships.

This window helps you better comprehend the relationships or connections between tables. To make finding content easier, it also lists every field in every table. You can produce

64

a report from the Relationships pane that documents a portion of your database design.

Give It a Try

- In the Relationships group, select Relationships after selecting the Database Tools option.
- The tables' current relationships will be displayed.
- Click Show Table in the Relationships group on the Relationship Tools: Design tab to bring up the Show Table dialog box.
- To add the table, double-click Personal Details, and then select [Close].

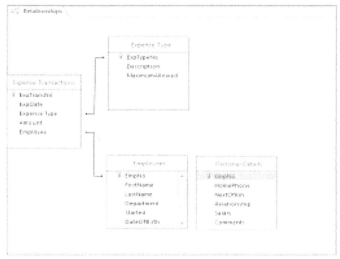

- The lines that show the table relationships are join lines.
- Drag the tables into place as shown using the mouse.

65

- Close the Relationships window after saving it.

COMMUNICATION OF TABLE JOINS

Although linking tables in a relational database in Microsoft Access is a simple process, some consideration should be given to the joins before they are made. There are four tables in our case study that must be connected. Before moving any farther, it is helpful to have a basic understanding of the kinds of joins we require and the reasons behind their use.

The quickest method for creating a relationship is to move the mouse pointer from one field in one table to another field in another table while the Relationships window is open.

66

It's a really basic and straightforward approach. For instance, the architecture of our expenses system includes two tables: one with information about our employees (Employees) and another with expense transactions (Expense Transactions).

By using the EmpNo number as a code to search for the employee data in the Employees table, this structure makes sure that we don't have to enter the employee details again each time an employee has an expense to report.

Let's pause and think about our actions. We are informing Microsoft Access that there will be a single employee record in Employees and numerous in Expense Transactions as a result of this interaction. EmpNo is a common field between the two tables. Since the EmpNo field is the primary key in the Employees table, it is unique and each employee can

67

only have one EmpNo number (keep in mind that it has a key icon because it is the primary key).

We are establishing a one-to-many relationship from a design standpoint. The link field in the single table needs to be the primary key in order to accomplish this. In the many table, the link field is referred to as the foreign key.

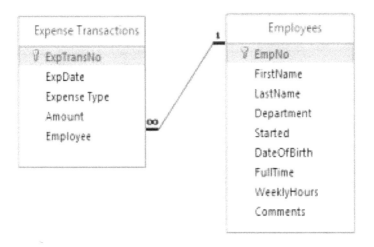

In Microsoft Access, a line is drawn between the two tables' relevant fields when a join is made. The type of join is indicated by the symbols on the line. The Employees' table is a one table, but the Expense Transactions table is a many table, as indicated by the infinity symbol. Here are a few more things to think about. Should referential integrity be enforced? The answer is yes if we wish to prevent the creation of an expense record that

68

isn't connected to an active employee. Do we want all of the EmpNo numbers in expenditures to update when we alter the EmpNo in Employees if we choose referential integrity? We need to activate the Cascade Update if the response is affirmative.

Once more, Cascade Delete must be enabled if we wish to remove every expense associated with an employee when we remove them from the Employees database. It goes without saying that these inquiries must be made for each join we make between every table in the system.

69

CHAPTER EIGHT

EDITING THE JOIN IN THE EMPLOYEE TABLE

The standard join parameters are used for joins made with the Lookup Wizard. However, they lack any parameters for referential integrity. To ensure integrity between the tables, you must use the Relationships window to modify the join. We want to make sure that the Employees table reflects any revisions in our case study.

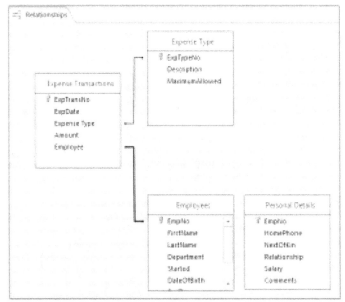

Give It a Try

- Click on Relationships in the Relationships group on the Database Tools tab.

70

- To pick the join line between the Employees and Expense Transactions tables, click on it; it should look a little thicker.
- To open the Edit Relationships dialog box, select Edit Relationships from the Tools group on the Relationship Tools: Design tab.

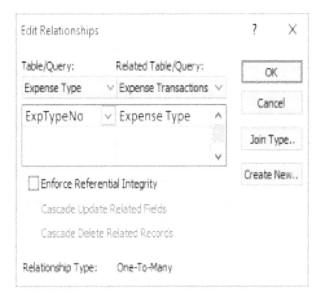

- Press Enforce Referential Integrity until a checkmark appears.
- Select Cascade Update Related Fields and wait for a checkmark to appear.

- Make sure there is no checkmark next to Cascade Delete Related Fields.
- Click [OK] to make the changes take effect.
- A one-to-many relationship is indicated by the symbols on the join.
- Close the window for relationships.

EDITING THE TABLE JOIN FOR EXPENSE TYPE

For the join between the Expense Transactions and Expense Type tables, we should also configure the referential integrity parameters.

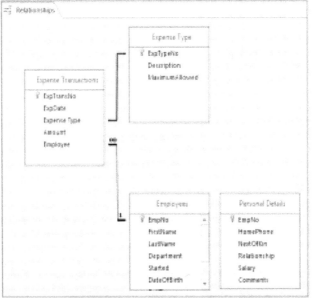

Referential integrity will guarantee that we cannot add a record to the transactions table without a corresponding

72

entity in the lookup table because these tables have a one-to-many relationship.

Give It a Try

- Click on All Relationships under the Relationships group on the Database Tools tab.

- To choose it, click the join line that connects the Expense Transactions and Expense Type tables; it should look a little thicker.

- To open the Edit Relationships dialog box, select Edit Relationships from the Tools group on the Relationship Tools: Design tab.

- Press Enforce Referential Integrity until a checkmark appears.

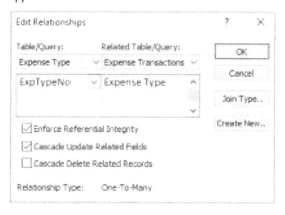

- Select "Cascade." Modify the Related Fields until a checkmark appears.

73

- Make sure the Cascade Delete Related fields don't have a checkmark.

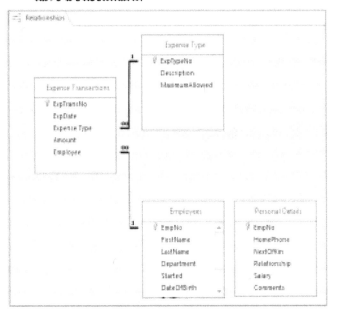

DEVELOPING A REPORT ON RELATIONSHIPS

It is advisable to document your table associations after they have all been established and adjusted to your satisfaction. Using the Relationships box, you can create a Relationship Report, which is actually the relationships window's print preview. You can then print this on paper or a file for documentation purposes.

74

Give It a Try

- Click on Relationships in the Relationships group on the Database Tools tab.
- To generate a report of the relationships, select Relationship Report from the Tools group on the Relationship Tools: Design tab.

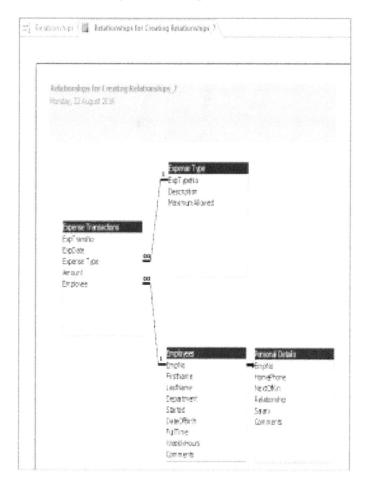

75

- The report shows up in the database window as an additional tab.
- Click Print in the Print group on the Print Preview tab to bring up the Print dialog box.
- Click [OK] after making sure your printer is online

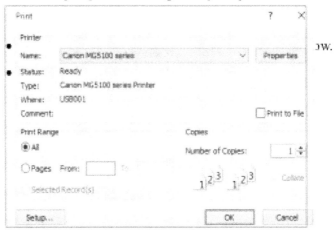

Databases must be updated on a regular basis. Prices fluctuate, customers move, and occasionally inaccurate data is entered into a database. Modifying existing data is comparatively simple using Microsoft Access. Editing is the term used in computer lingo to describe making changes to data. Access is a complete database management solution

76

that lets you add, update, and remove data. Either a form or Datasheet view, which displays your data in rows and columns on the screen, can be used for this.

EXAMINING A FIELD

For a general search of the entire table, utilize the Search box located at the bottom of a Datasheet window. Access offers additional, more focused search options for looking within a field. To access these tools, right-click on a field heading to bring up the shortcut menu, and then choose Find to bring up the Find What dialog box.

Give It a Try

- To open the Employees table, double-click on it.
- To open the Find and Replace dialog box, right-click on the header of the Last Name field and choose Find.
- To see the first occurrence, type Smith into Find What and then select [Find Next].

77

- After selecting [Find Next] to show the subsequent instance, observe how a notification stating that no more matching records are available displays.

- After selecting [OK], click the drop arrow for Match in the Find and Replace dialog box, then choose Any Part of the Field.

- After selecting [Find Next], you will see that "Smith" has been located.
- To exit the Find and Replace dialog box, click [Cancel].
- Shut down the table.

OUTPUTTING DATA FROM A TABLE

Data can be taken out of your database and put on paper in a number of ways. Nonetheless, there are two primary

methods: either print the list of records from an open table or create a report object in the database.

The simpler method, printing records straight from a table, will be covered in this section.

Give It a Try

- To open the Employees table, double-click on it. To view the Backstage, select the File tab.

79

- To view the Print section, click Print.

- To open the Print dialog box, click Print.

- Click [OK] after making sure your printer is online and prepared to print.

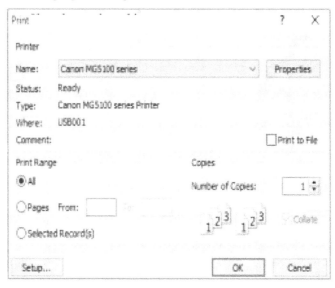

CHAPTER NINE

PACKAGING A DATASET

Changes and deletions made to a table are instantly visible to you on the screen, but hidden data and information remain hidden in the table's nooks and crannies.

For best performance, Access has a compacting and mending tool that fixes and resizes table data as well as does basic cleanup.

Give It a Try

To view the Backstage, click the File tab, then make sure Info is chosen. [Compact & Repair Database] is clicked. Because the compaction procedure works rapidly and, in the background, it will appear as though nothing has happened.

TABLES FORMATTING

Formatting is the process of altering something's appearance, usually to make it easier to read or more aesthetically beautiful. Access's default table formatting is quite boring. Thankfully, Access offers a variety of table formatting capabilities, such as the ability to alter typefaces and font colors, shade the background of cells, and change the gridlines between columns and rows.

Simple reports of the data can be created and printed quickly and effectively by designing a table because tables are easy to print.

EDITING FONTS

Access displays your data in a Datasheet using a selection of standard fonts, but you can use almost any font that is present on your machine. You may apply colored fonts, change the

82

font sizes, and do a lot more. For the sake of accuracy, it is crucial to pick a typeface that is easy to read.

- To view a color palette, select the Font Color drop arrow in the Text Formatting group on the Home tab.
- To alter the font's color, click on Dark Blue in Standard Colors (column 4, row 1).
- To enlarge the font size, click the down arrow for Font Size and select 16.

A bit too much to handle...

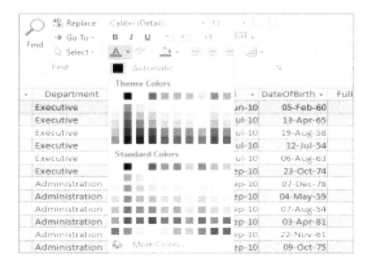

- To reduce the font size, click the down arrow for Font Size and then select 10. It's a little small now.
- Increase the text size to 11 and repeat.

83

- To alter the font, select Book Antiqua by clicking on the Font drop arrow.

Let's reverse this.

- To return the font to Calibri (Detail), repeat.
- Close and save the table.

FILTERING DATES

It can be a little challenging to apply filters to dates. Generally speaking, you want to filter on a range of dates rather than a single date.

For instance, you might want to view every individual who began in December 2007 in our case study. You would need to filter between December 1 and December 31 in order to accomplish this. The Between Dates filter option can be used for this.

Department ▾	PhoneNo ▾	Started ▾	DateOfBirth ▾	Ful
Executive	75001	28-Jun-10	05-Feb-60	
Executive	75002	19-Jul-10	13-Apr-65	
Executive	75005	19-Jul-10	06-Aug-63	
Administratio	61027	06-Sep-10	22-Nov-61	
Sales & Marke	63018	09-Dec-10	25-May-64	
Sales & Marke	63002	06-Nov-10	08-Jul-62	
Sales & Marke	63013	02-Dec-10	06-Dec-62	
Sales & Marke	63028	16-Dec-10	14-Jul-65	
Sales & Marke	63003	06-Nov-10	03-Sep-64	
Sales & Marke	63029	16-Dec-10	23-Feb-63	

84

- Click in any DateOfBirth field after double-clicking the Employees table to access it.
- To view the filter menu, select Filter from the Sort & Filter group on the Home tab.

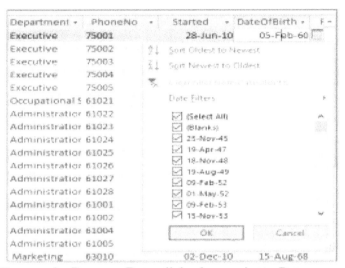

- To open the Between Dates dialog box, point to Date Filters and choose Between.
- Enter 01-Jan-60 in Oldest, then twice press Tab to enter 31-Dec-65 in Newest.
- To view every employee who was born between 1960 and 1965, click [OK].

85

- To remove the modifications, click [No] to close the table.

RECORD EXPORTATION TO MICROSOFT EXCEL

Since Microsoft Excel and Microsoft Access are part of the same product suite, exporting data is simple and almost trivial. The integrated Export Wizard automatically turns Access records into rows and fields from an Access database into columns. This makes it possible to export the data to an Excel worksheet with ease.

- Double-clicking the Employees – Administration table in the Navigation pane will open it.

- To open the Export Wizard, select Excel from the Export group after selecting the External Data tab.

- Here, you can provide the path and name of the destination file.

- After selecting [Browse], find and double-click the course files folder.

The file name that appears by default will be used.

- To execute the export and bring up the Save Export Steps option in the wizard, click [Save] and then [OK].
- To return to the table, click [Close] after making sure the Save export steps are displayed without a checkmark.
- Shut down the table.

RECORD EXPORTATION TO A TEXT FILE

The foundation of data import and export is text files. Text file types can be imported and exported from almost any application that contains data. Therefore, you can export Access records as text and then import them into the destination application if you want to send them to an application that isn't listed in the export options.

LAUNCH THE SALES-EMPLOYEES TABLE

- To open the Export Wizard, select the External Data tab and then select Text File from the Export group. There are a few extra procedures involved in exporting to text.
- After selecting the course files folder by clicking [Browse], click [Save] to choose the destination, and then click [OK].

88

- Click [Next] to specify the delimiter character after making sure Delimited is selected.

- After making sure the comma is chosen as the delimiter, click [Next].

- The proposed filename will be used. To bring up the Save Export Steps option in the wizard, click [Finish].

- Click [Close] after making sure the Save export steps are displayed without a checkmark.

- Shut down the table.

CHAPTER TEN

DEVELOPING AND APPLYING FORMS

Data in tables, queries, and reports can be accessed more readily because to the user-friendly interface that forms offer. For users with little experience with Access, they can be used to automate procedures, offer a navigation system, and overall make life easier.

COMPREHENDING FORMS

Data that would typically be displayed in rows and columns in a table can be made more aesthetically pleasing on the screen by using forms, which are essentially unique templates. Forms can be used to add new data, change existing data, and examine data on the screen. You can easily design forms from scratch, using an existing database as a basis, or by following a unique Wizard that guides you through the process.

MAKING FORMS

It's not hard to work with records in tables. Opening a table and letting people work directly at it, however, might lead to a number of issues. They might unintentionally erase documents, tamper with data in fields, or even view some data fields (such pay details) that you would prefer they

90

didn't. By giving users access to the data through forms, you can manage what they see and work with rather than giving them direct access to the data in a table.

Forms are designed to serve as structural templates into which data is inserted when the form is viewed; they do not themselves contain data. In essence, the template specifies what should be shown (such as which fields to utilize), where it should be shown (such as where the fields should be on the page), and how it should appear (such as font size, color, etc.).

A form is initially built using an existing table or query as its foundation. If you want to report on all of the data, you base the form on a table; if you want to display a portion of the data, you base it on a query.

THE VARIOUS METHODS FOR FORM CREATION

Access allows you to design both basic and extremely sophisticated forms. As you may anticipate, Access provides multiple forms creation options. The tools on the ribbon's construct tab are used to construct forms in Access. You can make:

- A simple form made with the Form, Split, or Multiple Items tools; these tools generate a form that appears

91

nearly instantaneously and requires minimal effort from you because they handle all the work.

- More complex forms can be constructed with the Form Wizard tool, which figuratively holds your hand while posing a series of questions that, when answered, cause the form to be generated for you according to your specifications.

- A complicated, elaborate form utilizing either the Blank Form tool or the Form Design tool — these options present you with a blank form canvas and you are needed to do all of the work to lay out what you want, where you want it, and how it should look. Because you have to handle everything yourself, this is the most challenging choice to utilize.

REACHING EQUILIBRIUM

There is no right or incorrect way to develop forms; instead, pick the approach that uses the least amount of time and effort to produce the desired results.

The best thing about Access's form creation tools is that, even after you've created a form using any of the aforementioned methods, you can still edit and customize it to exactly what you want. Therefore, you can still alter the form design yourself even if the Form Wizard hasn't done

92

everything it should or the basic form doesn't quite give you what you want.

A lot of Access users start by creating their forms with the Form, Split Form, or Form Wizard tools, then modify the layout or design to fit their requirements.

CONSTRUCTING A SIMPLE FORM

The Form tool, located on the build tab of the ribbon, is among the most straightforward and easy ways to build a form in Access. Simply choose the table or query that will serve as the form's foundation, then click the tool. This method works well for displaying a form on the screen instantly for revision or data entry.

- You MUST open the Creating Forms file before beginning this activity.
- To choose which table to utilize, click on the Employees table in the Navigation pane.
- After selecting the Create tab, select Form from the Forms group.
- A form layout will show up right away. You can modify the form template using the layout view of the form.

93

- To view the form in Form View where the data is shown, click on the upper portion of View in the Views group.

- To navigate through the records, click on the different Record buttons in the Navigation bar at the bottom of the screen.

- To bring up the Save As dialog box in the QAT, click Save.

- To save the form, enter frmEmployees in the Form Name field and select [OK].

- Shut down the form.

FORMATION OF A SPLIT

A split form is another simple and quick form that you may make with Access. A split form displays a datasheet view at the bottom of the screen and a regular form at the top, where only one record is displayed at a time. The records are displayed in a table fashion on the datasheet. The fields for a record are displayed in the top form each time you click on it in the datasheet.

- You can either open the file or continue using the prior file for this experiment.

94

MAKING FORMS

- Click on the Employees table in the Navigation pane. After choosing the Create tab, pick Split Form by clicking on More Forms in the Forms group.

- A split form layout will show up right away. To view the form in Form View, select View from the Views group on the Form Layout Tools: Design menu.

- In the navigation bar, click the record buttons. Click EmpNo to bring up the information in the top form.

- To bring up the Save As dialog box in the QAT, click Save.

- Click [OK] after entering frmEmployeesSplitForm in the Form Name field.

- Shut down the form.

HOW TO USE THE FORM WIZARD

You can use the Form Wizard to construct a form, giving you more control over what should be on it and how it should appear. You can create a new form by following the instructions provided by the Form Wizard. Each of the screens in the Form Wizard asks you to define which fields to include, how the form should appear, and what the new form should be called.

95

- Click on the Employees table in the Navigation pane. To launch the wizard, click the Create tab and then select Form Wizard from the Forms group. EmpNo, FirstName, LastName, Department, and PhoneNo can be added to the list of Selected Fields by double-clicking on them.
- To move on to the next screen, click [Next]. Then, use the settings as indicated to continue working through the displays.
- Click [Finish] to build the form after you have entered the title in the wizard's final screen.
- Shut down the form.

CHANGING THE FORMS

In Access, forms are mostly used to show data from tables or queries on the screen. The Access form generation tools are typically used to create forms, which are subsequently adjusted to meet particular needs. From altering the color palette to totally redesigning the form's style and functionality, this change might take many different forms. You will be making numerous changes to a standard form that was previously made using the form generator throughout this session.

Special Note: The creation and modification of forms and reports are very comparable. Both employ a template method in which the layout and design are defined by means of unique placeholders called controls that indicate the locations of data. You will be able to use a lot of the abilities and information you learn in this session for both forms and reports.

COMPREHENDING THE LAYOUT AND DESIGN OF FORMS

Even while you could make your own forms from the ground up, it would take a lot of work. Even experienced Access programmers use the form building tools to create a basic form, which they subsequently alter and adjust to meet their unique needs. Although changing a form is not difficult, you should first grasp a few conceptual concepts.

Templates are forms. Even though the term "template" has a wide range of often specialized meanings in the computing industry, it does an excellent job of describing what a form actually is. What should display on the screen, where it should appear, and how it should appear are all determined by the elements on a form, which is essentially a template. The headline, logos, data placeholders, and even the background are all objects on a form.

ITEMS ON THE FORM

Each item on the form has qualities that dictate its appearance (format), content (data), and behavior (event). This includes the form itself, which is an object. Data from a table, query, or expression (formula) is shown in a form using a unique kind of object called a control. Controls can be unbound and display either static (like a heading) or dynamic (like the current date) data, or they can be connected to a data source (like a field from a database). Therefore, modifying a form involves experimenting with its objects, such as scaling them, adding more, removing ones that aren't needed, altering their typefaces or colors, etc.

THE THREE FORM PERSPECTIVES

A form can be viewed in three different ways. A form will launch when you double-click on it in the Navigation pane. Data from the data source (such as a table or query) is combined into the controls on the form template and shown on the screen when the form is in operation. This view is what your database's users will use to view their data. Additionally, you can alter the form using the Layout View and Design View views. You may reposition objects and modify their characteristics in each of these views to customize how they seem and act.

More akin to a layout preview is Layout View. Your controls will display with data in Layout View exactly as they would if the form were active. Because the controls already contain data—from the first record—you may change them, resize, recolor, and move them around to see precisely how they will look when the form is executed.

The majority of the layout and cosmetic adjustments that can be made in Layout View can also be made in Design View. Additionally, you can add controls and fine-tune all of the control settings. The titles of the controls, not the actual data,

99

are displayed in Design View together with the form's header, body, and footer sections.

CHOOSING THE FORM OBJECTS

An object is anything that is visible on a form, including

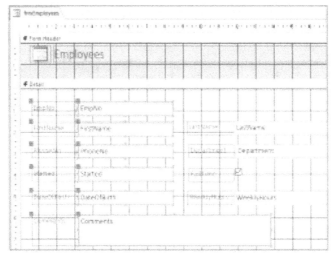

the form itself. You must first choose the object you want to work with in both Design View and Layout View before you can do anything with it. Typically, all it takes to choose an object is a mouse click. An object that has been selected will show up with a colored border to show that it is the active object.

ALIGNING CONTROLS

You'll realize how challenging it may be to align controls once you begin moving them across a form. You will require patience and strong coordination if you try to align controls

100

with your eye and the mouse. Thankfully, aligning controls is made simple by a number of alignment tools available on the ribbon's Arrange tab.

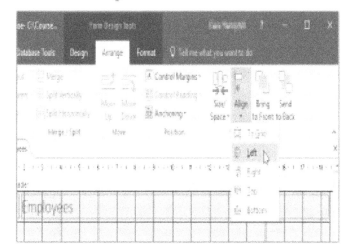

- Open frm Employees in Design View To choose the controls, hold down and click on them as indicated.
- To align the controls along their left sides, click the Form Design Tools: Arrange tab, then select Align from the Sizing & Ordering group.
- As indicated, click FirstName, then hold down to click on the remaining controls in the row. To align the controls horizontally, click Align in the Sizing & Ordering group on the Form Design Tools: Arrange tab, then choose Bottom.

101

- Using the previously mentioned procedures, align each horizontal row to the bottom, the EmpNo and LastName columns of labels to the left.

- If necessary, space controls horizontally with the arrow keys.

- Close and save the form.

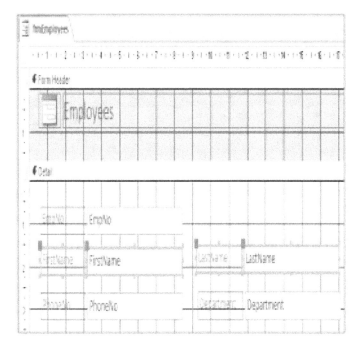

COMPREHENDING ASPECTS

The form itself is an object, as is everything else on it, and all objects have qualities that may be changed. While some items may have hundreds of attributes, others may just have

102

a few. An object's properties determine its appearance, behavior, and actual function.

GETTING TO THE OBJECT PROPERTIES

Particularly when it comes to properties and how they are accessed, there are typically several ways to accomplish the same goal with Access. For instance, using the commands on the ribbon is the most obvious approach to alter the font of a control. But when you use these commands to alter an item's appearance or behavior, you are actually altering some aspects of that object. It is frequently simpler to open the Property Sheet pane and modify the settings using the appropriate property rather than looking for the correct command.

COMPREHENDING THE PROPERTY SHEET PANE

The properties of the currently selected object in the form are shown in the Property Sheet window. The properties of the form itself are shown if no object is selected. Each of the five tabs that make up the Property Sheet pane shows a different set of settings. Format, Data, Event, and Other are the four distinct tabs: the settings from all four tabs are shown on the fifth tab:

- The Format tab shows the control's appearance settings, such as font, color, and height.

103

- When applicable, the Data tab's options link the object to a data source (such as a table's field).

- The options on the Event tab control how that object will act, such as when it is clicked or altered.

- Settings that don't belong in the other three categories are included in the Other tab.

- There is a lot of information about the object you are now selecting in the Property Sheet pane.

FORMING QUESTIONS

Table sorting and filtering options make it simple to find and sort data. But compared to utilizing queries, these are rather light.

Query By Example, or QBE, is another name for queries. A report based on the information in a database is similar to a query. When using a query, you must indicate which records to display and which fields to see. As with a basic filter, this is accomplished by providing Access with criteria to look for. Examples of queries include displaying all records with Sales in the Department field or all records pertaining to December 3. Access will search through the data and generate a table of entries that match once the criteria and output fields have been designated.

105

CHAPTER ELEVEN

COMPREHENDING QUERY

Using a select query is similar to applying a filter to your data so that you only see the information that matters to you. For instance, you can use select queries to generate a list of Tasmanian clients or a list of every item you've bought for $300 or more in the previous six months. Because they choose records based on your query design, select queries get their name. The ribbon's build tab is used to build select queries, which are then executed and edited in the Navigation pane as Query objects. A Query Design serves as the foundation for certain inquiries. The Query Grid is the lowest component of the design, and the Field List is the upper part.

QUERY GRID WITH A FIELD LIST

The procedure is sometimes called "query by example" because the records that are shown in the query are based on the sample data that you insert into the Criteria row in the Query Grid. Changing to Datasheet view is the simplest way to view the data. The data that meets the query criteria is shown in a unique dynaset table in Datasheet view. Although a dynaset is a subset of the entire table of data, it is still a live

106

set, and any modifications performed here will eventually be reflected in the full database.

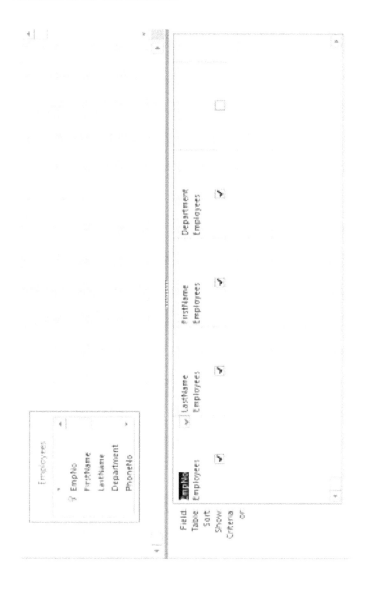

107

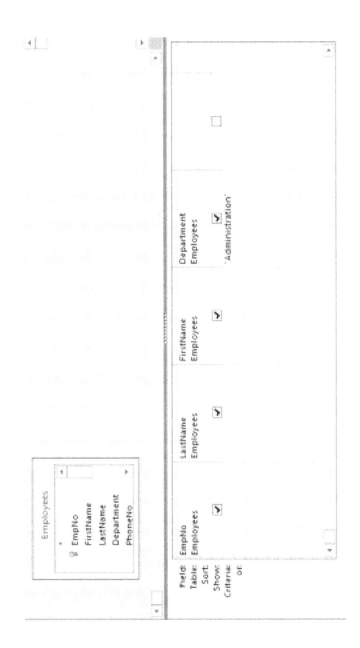

108

MAKING A DESIGN FOR A QUERY

The ribbon's Create tab is where queries are made. Similar to table structures, there is a run view where the data is imported from the appropriate table into the design layout structure, and a design view where the layout, criteria, and other elements needed for the query are given. Therefore, developing a query design structure is the first step in developing a query.

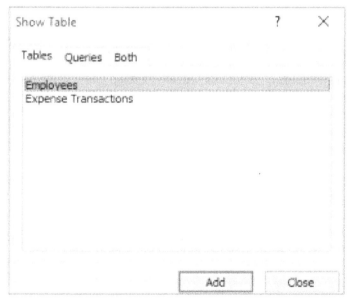

- To view a new query design and the Show Table dialog box, select the Create tab and then select Query Design from the Queries group.

109

- To include the Employees table fields in the design, click [Add].
- To exit the dialog box, click [Close]. Double-clicking EmpNo, LastName, FirstName, and Department in the field listing will add them to the grid in that order.
- To bring up the Save As dialog box in the QAT, click Save.
- Click [OK] after typing qryEmployees into the Query Name field.
- The query name will now show up in the Queries heading of the Navigation pane.
- Close the query.

USING THE RECORD CRITERIA

The ability of a query to show a filtered list of records in a dynaset is what gives it its true strength. You must input search criteria in the criterion row of the query grid in order to filter the records and view only the ones you desire.

To see all records from the original table that meet the criteria, just put an example of the data you wish to see in the criterion box and execute the query.

111

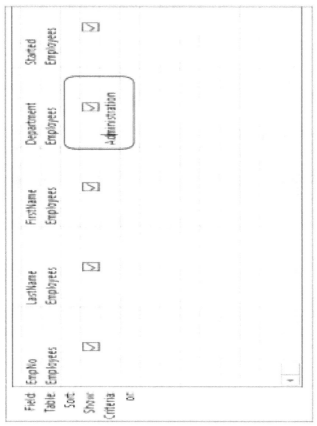

- To bring up a menu of options, right-click on qryEmployees and choose Design View.

- Click in the Department Criteria cell and select Administration.

- To view just entries with Administration in the Department field, click on the top half of View in the Views group on the Query Tools: Design tab.

112

- To return to Design view, repeat step 3 and type 40 in the WeeklyHours Criteria field. Then, click View to see just those employees who put in 40 hours in the Administration department.

- To view all administration employees who put in 40 hours and make at least $80,000, switch to Design view, enter >=80000 in the Criteria column for Salary, and then click View.

- Close and save the query.

DEFINING THE CRITERIA FOR SELECTION

When running queries, you do need to use some caution. You risk receiving inaccurate results if you leave leftover criteria from a previous query in the query grid, which is simple to

113

do if you have more fields than what can be visible on the screen. Clearing the selection criteria after running a query and locating the desired data is therefore a smart idea.

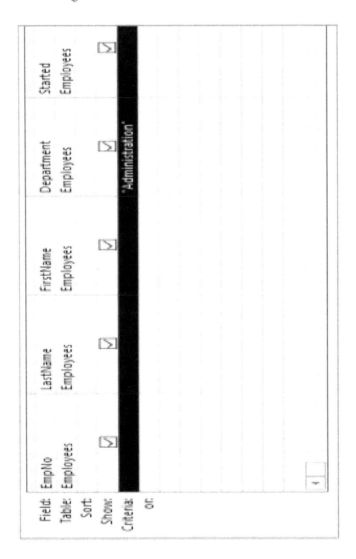

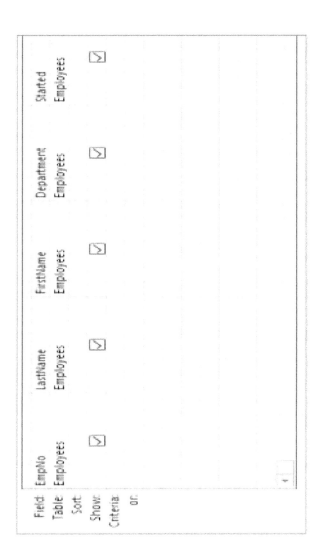

- Choose Design View Point to the left of the first criteria cell in the Navigation pane by right-clicking on qryEmployees to bring up a menu of options.

115

- Continue until the mouse pointer turns into a black horizontal arrow.
- To choose all of the criteria, click once. row
- To remove every criterion in the row, press Close and save the query.

REMOVING A QUERY

Data that is stored in tables or that comes from other inquiries is frequently used by queries. They can be used as a source of data for other inquiries, forms, and reports, as well as to generate data through calculations. As a result, you should exercise extra caution when deleting queries; first, be sure that no other objects in the database are using the query.

- To choose it, click on qryEmployeesExec in the Navigation pane.

- In the Records group on the Home tab, select Delete.
- A caution message asking for your permission to remove the query will show up.
- Select [Yes] to validate the removal.
- In the Navigation pane, the query is no longer listed under Queries.

117

CHAPTER TWELVE

FORMING AND APPLYING REPORTS

Data from tables or queries can be properly presented using Access reports. Reports are essentially used to display raw data in a way that is easier to read, comprehend, and visually appealing.

COMPREHENDING ACCESS REPORTING

You can more formally present and even analyze the data from your tables and searches with reports. Although reports have historically been created as printed documents, they can also be published online or read on a screen. It's best to know how they operate and what they can do for you before you start writing a report.

MAKING REPORTS

You can create reports using the report generator feature found in all database systems, including Access. Reports are designed as structural templates that, when run, incorporate data; they do not themselves contain data. In essence, the template specifies what should be shown (such as which fields to utilize), where it should be shown (such as where the fields should be on the page), and how it should appear (such as font size, color, etc.).

118

A report's initial creation is predicated on an already-existing table or query. If you want to report on all of the data, you base the report on a table; if you want to report on only a portion of the data, you base it on a query.

THE VARIOUS METHODS FOR WRITING A REPORT

You can construct both basic and extremely complicated reports in Access. As you may anticipate, Access provides a variety of report creation options. The tools on the produce tab of the ribbon in Access are used to produce reports. You can make:

- Using the Report tool, create a simple, straightforward report that takes very little effort on your part and appears very instantaneously. You have everything done for you.

- More complex reports can be created with the Report Wizard tool, which holds your hand in a metaphorical manner while posing a series of questions that, when answered, produce a report.

- A sophisticated, intricate report created with the Blank Report or Report Design tools; in these cases, you are given a blank report canvas and must do all the work to specify what you want, where you want

119

it, and how it should appear. Because you have to handle everything yourself, this is the most challenging choice to utilize.

REACHING EQUILIBRIUM

There is no right or wrong way to prepare reports; instead, pick the approach that uses the least amount of time and effort to produce the desired outcomes.

The best thing about Access's reporting capabilities is that you can still edit, modify, and customize them to exactly what you want after creating a report using any of the approaches. Therefore, you can still alter the report design yourself even if the basic report doesn't quite provide you what you need or the Report Wizard hasn't done what it should. A lot of Access users utilize the Report tool or the Report Wizard tool to build their reports, then modify the layout or design to fit their requirements.

FORMING A SIMPLE REPORT

Using the Report tool, which is found on the Create tab of the ribbon, is the quickest and most straightforward method for creating a basic report in Access. Here, all you have to do is run the command after choosing the table or query in the Navigation pane to serve as the report's foundation.

120

THE REPORT WIZARD'S USE

You can create more formal reports using the data in your data table by following the instructions provided by the Report Wizard. The Report Wizard is made up of several windows that ask you for the data needed to create a report. At first, some of the displays could appear confusing, but

you will quickly understand what is needed and be able to produce reports effectively.

- To choose the table to report on, click on the Employees table in the Navigation pane.
- To launch the Report Wizard, select the Create tab and then select Report Wizard from the Reports group.

121

- To include EmpNo, FirstName, LastName, Department, and PhoneNo in the list of Selected Fields, double-click on them in the Available Fields.

- To move on to the following screen, click [Next].

- Use the parameters as indicated to continue navigating the panels.

- After selecting the title on the wizard's final screen, click Preview the report and then [Finish] to begin creating the report.

- Take a moment to look at the report.

- End the report.

The Navigation pane now displays the updated report.

FORMING A REPORT IN GROUP

You can display data in a grouped report by grouping it based on one or more fields. For instance, the departments and the employees within each department will be listed alphabetically if you build a grouped report that lists all employees by department.

- Click on the Employees table in the Navigation pane.
- To launch the Wizard, select the Report Wizard under the Reports group after selecting the Create tab.
- Click [Next] after double-clicking on Department, EmpNo, LastName, FirstName, Started, and Salary.

123

- You must indicate how to group the records on this screen.
- Select the Department grouping level by double-clicking on it.
- After selecting [Next], proceed with the next wizard screens as instructed.
- Press [Finish] to create the report.
- End the report.

124

CHAPTER THIRTEEN

WORKING WITH REPORTS GROUPED

Access will use cryptic symbols, such as the hash (#) symbol, to replace data if a column is too narrow to display values. This may occur when values including numerous numbers, like currency, are subjected to statistical procedures (sum, average, etc.). You must adjust the column widths in Layout View or Design View in order to fix this issue.

- Double-clicking Salary Analysis Report in the Navigation pane will launch it.

125

- Here, the numbers are replaced by hash signs.
- Navigate to Design View.
- Click on =Sum([Sal] in the Department Footer, then hold down and choose =Avg([Sal, =Min([Sal, =Max([Sal and =Sum([Sal) (in Report Footer)).
- You ought to have chosen five fields.
- Point to one of the chosen fields' left borders, then click and drag to the left until the fields are roughly three times as long.
- To run the report, click the Home tab, then select the Views group's bottom half, and finally choose
- Report View. This time, the data are shown.
- Close and save the report.

FORMING A REPORT WITH STATISTICS

The ability to summarize database data is a fantastic feature of reports. Reports, for instance, let you determine the number of records (count), minimum, maximum, average, and total (sum) for numerical columns in a database. Additionally, non-numerical fields can be counted. These statistical reports aid in the database's data analysis.

- Click the Employees table in the Navigation pane, then select the Create tab and Report Wizard under the Reports group.

126

- Click [Next] after double-clicking on Department and Salary.

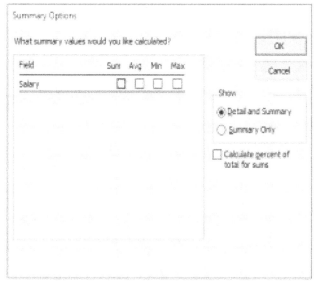

- Click [Next] after double-clicking Department as the Grouping level.

- To open the Summary Options dialog box, click [Summary Options].

- After selecting the checkboxes for Sum, Avg, Min, and Max, select Summary Only under Show.

- To return to the Wizard, click [OK]. Then, click [Next] and finish the settings as indicated.

- Press [Finish] to create the report.

- The hash signs will be fixed in the upcoming exercise.

127

- End the report.

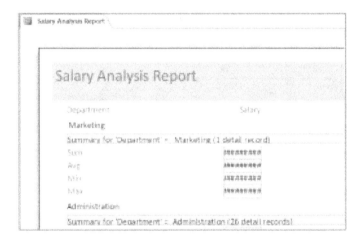

CONCLUSION

In today's data-driven world, mastering Microsoft Access empowers you to transform raw information into actionable insights. Throughout this journey, you've explored the core functions and advanced capabilities of Access, equipping yourself with the skills to design, manage, and optimize databases tailored to your unique needs.

Whether you're a beginner laying the groundwork or an experienced user seeking to refine your expertise, this book has provided you with practical exercises and diverse examples to reinforce your learning. Remember, the key to becoming proficient lies in continued practice and exploration.

As you move forward, utilize the concepts and techniques you've learned to tackle real-world data challenges confidently. With Access as your ally, you can streamline your data processes, enhance collaboration, and ultimately make informed decisions that drive success.

Thank you for embarking on this journey with us. Here's to your continued growth and innovation in the realm of database management!

NOTE